Original title:
The Grove of Giggles

Copyright © 2025 Creative Arts Management OÜ
All rights reserved.

Author: Natalia Harrington
ISBN HARDBACK: 978-1-80567-192-3
ISBN PAPERBACK: 978-1-80567-491-7

A Tickle in the Air

Laughter dances, bright and clear,
Whispers of joy are all you hear.
Butterflies with silly grins,
Tumble down as fun begins.

Silly hats upon our heads,
Bouncing like we're made of spreads.
Jokes unfold like paper planes,
Soaring high through giggly chains.

The Harmony of Hilarity

Cuckoo birds tweet quirky tunes,
While squirrels juggle spoons and prunes.
Frogs in bow ties leap and croak,
Each jump a giggle, every poke.

Bouncing balls that chime and ring,
Silly dances make us swing.
Side-splitting stories shared at dusk,
In this haven, we feel the brisk.

Chucklewood Chronicles

Wobbly trees with wobbly jokes,
Each branch a tale of giggling folks.
Swaying together, hearts set free,
In this place of pure, wild glee.

Nuts and acorns form a band,
Playing tunes that are quite grand.
Spinning around, the world is bright,
In laughter's embrace, we take flight.

Radiant Revelations

Bubbles float in shimmering skies,
Tickling noses, bright surprise.
Jellybeans rolling on the ground,
With each bounce, new giggles found.

Puppies chase their bouncing tails,
As joyful laughter never fails.
Sunny rays that paint a grin,
Echo the joy that swells within.

Whispers of Laughter

In shadows soft, the chortles bloom,
Where squirrels dance, dispelling gloom.
The tickles of wind, a playful tease,
As giggles bounce through swaying trees.

A frog in a hat croaks quite absurd,
While butterflies flit, all softly stirred.
Each leaf a smile, each branch a cheer,
In this silly spot, there's no room for fear.

Sunlit Secrets

Beneath the beams, the shadows play,
A puppy's leap makes wishes sway.
The sun winks down with a grin,
As whispers of joy begin to spin.

A ladybug perched, quite fancy dressed,
Strings of humor that never rest.
With each tickle of dappled light,
The world giggles softly, pure delight.

Treetops of Joy

In canopies where dreams take flight,
Tiny creatures laugh, oh what a sight!
A raccoon juggles acorns with flair,
While cheeky monkeys hang with care.

Amidst the blooms, a chatter grows,
With silly stories only nature knows.
The breeze joins in, whirling about,
A symphony of chuckles, no doubt!

The Jester's Canopy

A jester's hat atop the trees,
Brings forth a rustle in the leaves.
He juggles stars, he flips the moon,
As night whispers, "Join the fun soon!"

With every glance, another jest,
As crickets croon, they do their best.
With antics wild and laughter loud,
Nature's stage is a joyous crowd.

Laughter's Radiance

In a grove of chuckles bright,
Where creatures dance in pure delight,
A squirrel spins with a silly hat,
While cats chase tails and a friendly rat.

Bouncing beans and giggling trees,
Whispering secrets on the breeze,
A jester leaps atop the stones,
With playful puns in cheerful tones.

Every leaf holds a vibrant jest,
As rabbits race, they're truly blessed,
The sun beams down, a warm embrace,
In this lively, joyful space.

So come and join this merry scene,
Where laughter reigns and all are keen,
A world of fun, where spirits soar,
In hues of laughter, forevermore!

The Fun-Filled Fables

In tales spun from sheer delight,
A dragon giggles, takes to flight,
With knights who trip on shiny shields,
And fairies who toss bright, silly yields.

Each fable twists with playful cheer,
A bear wearing glasses, oh so dear,
And wily foxes craft a plan,
With hiccuping gnomes and a bouncy span.

At twilight, shadows grow quite long,
As frogs croak out their evening song,
The moon, it winks with a refined glow,
While trickster stars put on a show.

So gather near, let laughter bloom,
In fables where joy erases gloom,
With every turn, a chuckle waits,
In the realm where fun captivates.

Sunshine Silhouettes

In sunlight's arms, where shadows play,
Silly shapes dance and sway,
A rabbit hops with a wink and grin,
While playful whispers swirl within.

Clouds like creams, all frothy white,
Cast silly forms in morning light,
As kids in laughter, roam around,
Chasing giggles, joy unbound.

Bright butterflies prance with glee,
While daisies giggle merrily,
And every step on the soft green grass,
Unfolds a tale where smiles surpass.

So frolic forth, embrace the light,
Where humor thrives and hearts take flight,
In the warmth of sunbeam's kiss,
Find the joy that you won't miss!

Festive Frolics in the Forest

In the woods where laughter grows,
Silly shadows dance in rows.
Squirrels wear hats and twirl around,
While the trees chuckle without a sound.

Bunnies bounce with giggly glee,
Tickling leaves on every spree.
Jokes are shared from twig to twig,
As nature joins in, big and big.

Radiant Ripples of Joy

By the brook, where sunshine plays,
Frogs croak funny in wild ways.
They splash with style, a frothy cheer,
Echoes of happiness fill the sphere.

Jellybeans fall from fluffy clouds,
As rabbits hop in giggling crowds.
Joyful whispers on every shore,
Make the heart dance and soar.

Sprout of Smirks

In a patch where grins sprout high,
Ticklish leaves whisper, 'Oh my!'
Branches bow to the clownish breeze,
Bending low with teasing ease.

Frilly flowers don grand smiles,
Cheering up the wandering miles.
With every step, there's boundless cheer,
As goofy antics draw us near.

The Playful Pathway

A winding path with joy anew,
Where whispers of giggles float right through.
Dancing shoes on froggy feet,
A silly tune, a rhythmic beat.

Lizards wear sunglasses, looking fine,
While butterflies sip sweet nectar wine.
Laughter twirls around each bend,
With every corner, smiles extend.

Playful Breezes

Whispers dance in the air,
Laughter floats with the breeze,
Tickled leaves in a playful flare,
Nature's giggles put me at ease.

Rustling branches play peek-a-boo,
Swaying in their silly cheer,
The sun joins in with a bright hue,
Turning the day into a dear.

Clouds chase each other up high,
Playing tag in a sky so blue,
With every swirl, the time flies,
Nature's playground come into view.

Every corner tells a jest,
In shadows where the sun hides,
A symphony of chuckles at best,
In this place where joy abides.

Joyful Murmurs of Nature

Birds chirp tales of delight,
Flowers dance in vibrant hues,
A symphony of pure sunlight,
Nature's joy spreads like shoes.

Merry mice scoot through the grass,
Sharing secrets with each flower,
A giggle here, a tickle there,
Every moment brings us power.

Gentle ripples laugh on streams,
Bouncing rocks play with the sun,
While frogs croak silly, joyous dreams,
In this realm where jokes are spun.

The world is a canvas so bright,
With colors dipped in vibrant glee,
Every leaf here takes flight,
In nature's riddle, we feel free.

Riddles in the Leaves

Leaves giggle with every breath,
Whispering secrets in plain sight,
Ticklish branches dance with death,
Waving hello, not a fright.

Breezes twist, the humor unfolds,
Each rustle a riddle to solve,
Nature's jokes, a treasure of gold,
In laughter, we freely dissolve.

Voices tease from every nook,
Telling tales of days gone by,
In the heart of this green book,
We find laughter, never shy.

Pinecones drop with a playful plop,
Squirrels scamper with delight,
In this realm, we never stop,
For the fun is truly out of sight.

Serendipity in Sunlight

Golden rays spill out the fun,
Dancing shadows sway on ground,
Bouncing bright like a playful pun,
In every twinkle, laughter found.

A tickle of warmth on my cheek,
As flowers lift their heads to greet,
Nature's beauty, never meek,
Produces giggles, so sweet.

Butterflies waltz in the air,
Wings flutter with joy and grace,
Every flutter beyond compare,
In this party, we all embrace.

Moments prance in sunlit plays,
Chasing dreams on this warm crest,
Eagerly dance through carefree days,
Finding cheer in nature's jest.

Frothy Fronds of Fun

In a land where chuckles grow,
Branches twist in gleeful flow.
Leaves shimmer with smiles so bright,
Tickles dance in morning light.

Breezes carry jokes untold,
In the sun, the stories bold.
Silly sprites jump and sing,
While the butterflies take wing.

Beneath the canopy of cheer,
Silly secrets waltz with deer.
Mirth spills from the rustling trees,
Carried softly on the breeze.

Laughter bubbles, pure delight,
Swaying shadows, day turns night.
In this realm where joy takes flight,
Every giggle feels just right.

Mirthful Murmurs

Whispers twirl on breezy trails,
Jovial tales of wobbly snails.
Giggling grasshoppers in a race,
Every jump a happy face.

Tickles roll on the grassy green,
Where the sunbeams play unseen.
Bouncing bunnies, bright and spry,
Chasing shadows in the sky.

Fluttering wings create a tune,
Urging flowers to join the swoon.
Clouds above with silver laughs,
Painting rainbows, joyful paths.

Echoes of chuckles 'round the bend,
Every smile a joyful friend.
In this haven of pure delight,
Mirthful murmurs soothe the night.

Whispers of Laughter

Soft echoes beneath the sun,
Where the jolly rivers run.
Tiny critters frolic near,
Belly laughs that bring good cheer.

Frogs in hats lead a parade,
With prancing paws that never fade.
Twiggy wands and giggly spells,
Mischief brewed in vibrant wells.

Every corner holds a grin,
Hiccups from a squirrel's kin.
Lemonade and giggles blend,
Refreshing fun that won't soon end.

Whispers spin like dandelion seeds,
Planting joy in playful deeds.
In the heart where laughter thrives,
Every moment brings it alive.

Echoes in the Meadow

Daisies dance with playful grace,
Bouncing off their own sweet space.
Hares that giggle, skip, and hop,
While lazy bees just buzz and plop.

Rainbow ribbons in the breeze,
Whirling whispers, tickling trees.
Clouds of fluff like candy cane,
Each burst of giggles we can't contain.

In between the grassy rows,
A symphony of laughter flows.
Nature's chorus sings along,
Creating joy in every song.

Echoes stretch to lands unknown,
Where the seeds of fun are sown.
In this playful, sunny glen,
Every mark of joy begins again.

Melodies in the Meadow

Beneath the bright and shining sun,
The flowers dance, they twirl for fun.
A breeze whispers jokes to the trees,
   Laughter echoes, carried with ease.

Butterflies laugh as they flit about,
They tease the bees, they buzz and shout.
Grasshoppers play their tiny drums,
While silly squirrels bounce with hums.

A rabbit hops, wearing a hat,
He trips on roots, and falls with a splat!
Everyone giggles, what a sight,
   In this meadow, all feels just right.

As dusk arrives with stars aglow,
The critters gather, putting on a show.
With every chuckle, joy fills the air,
A place where humor is everywhere.

Twinkling Lullabies

In the night, the fireflies gleam,
They wink and blink, what a dream!
A lullaby carried on the breeze,
With giggles hiding in the leaves.

Bunnies whisper tales of cheer,
While sleepy owls hoot near.
The world wraps softly in starlit care,
As snorts and chuckles fill the air.

Crickets join in, a quirky band,
With tiny violins in hand.
Laughter echoes through the glen,
A perfect night to dream again.

Slumber's embrace weaves gentle threads,
Of joyful giggles upon our beds.
In this space where laughter lies,
A twinkling world, beneath the skies.

The Ticklish Trail

On the path where giggles grow,
Tiny feet dance to and fro.
Tickling bushes, laughter spills,
As critters play with joyful thrills.

Wobbly hedgehogs roll and spin,
Chasing each other as they grin.
Silly stones trip the clumsy fox,
Who stumbles and laughs, oh what a paradox!

Bouncing badgers, full of glee,
Join a parade, just wait and see!
How a simple step can bring such mirth,
On the ticklish trail of delight and worth.

With every bend, a chuckle awaits,
Joyful pranks that the forest creates.
In this realm where fun prevails,
Life's a riot on ticklish trails.

Joyfulness Amidst the Boughs

Under boughs where shadows play,
Chirps and chuckles fill the day.
Squirrels play tag, between the trees,
In a world of laughter carried by the breeze.

A wise old owl winks his eye,
While rabbits tumble, oh my, oh my!
With every rustle, joy takes flight,
Mirthful moments shining bright.

The branches sway as the sun dips low,
Creating a dance, a soft glow.
Tickles float on the evening air,
With each giggle, burdens laid bare.

In this haven of sheer delight,
Where jesters frolic under moonlight,
Joyfulness wraps like a warm embrace,
In the laughter shared, we find our place.

Hilarity in Harmony

Beneath bright leaves that dance and sway,
Laughter echoes, weaving play.
Silly shadows leap and twirl,
In this joyful, giggling whirl.

A squirrel dressed like a clown,
Juggles acorns, upside down.
Birds chirp songs of pure delight,
As breezes join the merry fight.

Ticklish grass beneath our toes,
Where whimsy grows and nonsense flows.
Everyone's smiling, here and there,
In this place where none a care.

With every giggle, joy expands,
United here, in light-filled lands.
Let the world just fade away,
In hilarity, we choose to stay.

Boughs of Bliss

Up in branches, high and wide,
Laughter spills, no place to hide.
Breezes tickle the boughs so bright,
As squirrels dance, a comical sight.

Sunlight drips like honey sweet,
Through leafy paths, where friends all meet.
Every chuckle and every cheer,
Binds us close, away from fear.

With each rustle, a new jest flows,
In this land where mischief grows.
Playful shadows play tag and prance,
Inviting all to join the dance.

Amidst the giggles, worries wane,
Here, we cherish joy, not pain.
In this happy, frolicking space,
Every heart finds its perfect place.

Happiness in Hidden Corners

In the nooks where laughter hides,
Joyful secrets space abides.
Whispers of glee flutter about,
In these corners, there's no doubt.

Bouncing mushrooms, in a row,
Invite you to dance and glow.
A frog in socks, so bright and green,
Conducts a band, an unseen scene.

Underneath a floppy hat,
A doughnut rests, and oh, imagine that!
With every bite, a giggle bursts,
In these corners, laughter thirsts.

Friends encircle, hearts aligned,
In this crazy, friendly bind.
Every corner, every space,
Is filled with joy in every trace.

The Cheery Canopy

Underneath the bright green dome,
Where laughter makes a joyful home.
Picnics filled with silly games,
Every heart sings, not for fame.

Giggles echo, a playful song,
In this place where we belong.
Between the trees, a treasure hunt,
Where whimsy leads and laughter's blunt.

A dancing tree with wiggly limbs,
Joins our cheer with playful whims.
Ice cream drips and giggles soar,
In this canopy, there's always more.

With every smile, the world feels bright,
In this haven, pure delight.
So come along, and join the cheer,
In the cheery canopy, hold dear.

A Symphony of Chuckles

In a land where laughter grows,
Jolly pranks steal the show.
A trumpet blares, a tickle reigns,
Giggles echo through the lanes.

Bouncy trees with silly hats,
Dance along with playful cats.
A chorus of gaffes, a merry tune,
Joyful whispers beneath the moon.

Raccoons dressed as clowns arrive,
With pies in hand, they strive to thrive.
In this place, the silliness flows,
As choirs of chuckles paint the shows.

So come and join the frolic spree,
Where laughter's light sets spirits free.
With every smile, our worries wane,
In this symphony, delight we gain.

Petals of Playfulness

Amidst the blooms, a frolic fest,
Petals swirl with playful zest.
Sunny daisies dance around,
Tickling toes upon the ground.

Butterflies with mischief in mind,
Swoop and soar, laughter intertwined.
A giggle here, a chuckle there,
Joyous whispers fill the air.

Each flower shares a silly tale,
Of bouncing beans and happy whale.
In this field of smiles so bright,
We twirl and skip, pure delight.

Come, join the fun within this glade,
Where laughter blooms and worries fade.
With petals soft and hearts aglow,
Playfulness is sure to grow.

Echoes of Merriment

In the woods where giggles swell,
Echoes ring of stories to tell.
A squirrel slips, a tumble down,
As laughter spreads from town to town.

With every bend, a surprise awaits,
Bouncing rabbits on roller skates.
A joyous choir sings a refrain,
Of silly antics, time and again.

Whimsical whispers from the trees,
Invite you in with playful ease.
As shadows dance, and fireflies blink,
Join in the fun, don't you think?

With hearts so light and spirits high,
Let merriment reach for the sky.
In this echoing land of cheer,
Laughter brings everyone near.

Enchanted Laughter

In a glen where giggles bloom,
Magic forms in every room.
Frogs that croak a silly tune,
As butterflies waltz under the moon.

A jester sprawls on emerald grass,
Telling jokes that come to pass.
With every quip, a hearty laugh,
A world of play, our joyful craft.

Bright sunbeams tickle, shadows sway,
Whimsical antics lead the way.
A merry band of friends unite,
In this enchanted mood so bright.

With laughter shared and fun to keep,
Let's cherish moments rich and deep.
In this land of glee, we'll stay,
Where joy and laughter lead the play.

The Joyful Thicket

In a thicket of joy, where chuckles play,
Laughter twirls in the air, bright as day.
Bouncing rabbits wear hats, giggling so free,
A ticklish breeze whispers, come dance with me!

Beneath a bright tree, a squirrel can't sit,
He wiggles and jiggles, not caring a bit.
The mushrooms are grinning, their caps all aglow,
Joy bubbles over in this laughter show!

A parade of the ants, they strut with such flair,
While butterflies flutter, swirling in the air.
With jokes shared by bees, buzzing all around,
The thicket's alive with the silliest sound!

So come share a smile, let your giggles ring,
In this joyful thicket, you'll find everything.
A world where the funny and silly collide,
In laughter's embrace, let your worries subside.

Secrets Beneath the Leaves

Hidden secrets stir where the shadows play,
Whispers of giggles make dull moments sway.
A raccoon in glasses reads notes from the past,
While a wise old owl keeps the mischief steadfast.

Tickles of sunlight peek in from above,
While tricky old gnomes hide their sweets with love.
A squirrel may trip, with a comical thud,
And vines, they shake hands with the soft, warm mud.

With each rustle of leaves, a joke is retold,
The stories of laughter nostalgically unfold.
Pixies perform, with twirls and a spin,
Secrets of fun linger thick in the din!

So hush, my dear friend, come hear what they say,
In this world of whimsy, let troubles decay.
Underneath all the laughter, wisdom peeks through,
The secrets beneath are waiting for you!

Frolics in the Foliage

In the foliage thick, frolics abound,
Each leaf a stage, magic's found.
The jolly ol' fox plays peekaboo,
With giggles and chuckles, it's all quite a view!

Dancing dandelions sway in the breeze,
As crickets tell jokes, intent to please.
With frog-like leaps, they bound and they bop,
In this playful patch, there's never a stop!

The flowers are ticklish, they giggle in hues,
Swapping silly tales that bring hearty snooze.
A parade of the playful, oh what a sight,
From dawn until dusk, there's constant delight!

Under the sun's glow, let's join in the play,
Frolics in foliage, laughter on display.
So come share a moment, let joy be your guide,
In the playful world where humor resides.

The Laughing Glade

In a glade that chuckles, where shadows dance,
There's a bubbling creek, where giggles prance.
A jester, the crow in a hat too wide,
With a twinkle in his eye, spreads laughter worldwide!

The daisies are grinning, all in a row,
Bouncing to the rhythm, putting on a show.
A worm wearing glasses reads jokes from a tome,
Reporters of humor in this leafy dome!

Branch-bound buddies play hide and seek,
The fun doesn't end, it's all at its peak.
A gopher on roller skates zips by in a flash,
With cheers from the crowd, it's a glorious bash!

So wander in wonder, let mirth take its claim,
In the laughing glade, we're all part of the game.
With smiles that twinkle like stars up above,
This playful paradise is a treasure of love.

Cheerful Soiree of Shadows

In the nook where sillies play,
Laughter leaps and spins away.
Bouncing off the leafy floor,
Giggles peek behind the door.

Whispers dance with breezy tunes,
Tickling toes like happy loons.
Jesters hide and sprout anew,
In a world of shades and hue.

Chuckleberries grow on trees,
Frolic under buzzing bees.
A jolly parade, full of cheer,
Echoes through the bright frontier.

When shadows stretch and flicker bright,
Silly friends take flight at night.
With a giddy, glinting glow,
They cavort where few dare go.

Storytime in the Sunlight

Under beams that wink and gleam,
Silly tales flow like a dream.
A wise old owl with secrets wide,
Spills them forth with feathery pride.

The bunnies hop from tale to tale,
Spinning yarns beyond the pale.
With laughter bubbling every way,
A joyous, vibrant cabaret.

The sunbeams snicker, softly bright,
As characters take off in flight.
A dragon draped in rainbow hues,
Swirls about with wondrous views.

Every turn a chuckle brings,
In the realm where humor sings.
A tale that tickles every ear,
Leaves us giggling through the year.

Mischievous Meanderings

Little feet on trails of fun,
Skippy giggles, never done.
Chasing sunlight, dodging trees,
Silly games of tag with bees.

Rascals hide and peek-a-boo,
Squeaky voices laugh like dew.
Spinning round, they tumble down,
Rolling 'round in jolly gowns.

A tasty snack of sprightly cheer,
Imagined feasts appear right here.
Cupcakes spun from clouds above,
Filling hearts with giggling love.

Winks and nudges everywhere,
Each caught up in merry air.
Life a canvas full of flair,
With treasures hiding, bold and rare.

Revels in the Rustle

Amidst the leaves, a mischief stirs,
Squirrels plot and dance like furs.
Each rustle holds a playful jest,
Ticklish whispers, never rest.

Breezy breezes puff and tease,
Laughter floats upon the breeze.
Acorns tumble, plop, and fall,
Crazed critters heed the call.

Chirpy songs and hidden sights,
Gallivanting till the night.
A gathering of chuckles bright,
Encircled close with sheer delight.

In raucous cheer, the forest wakes,
As every ha-ha softly shakes.
An echo like a ringing bell,
In the rustle, laughter dwells.

Pranks of the Petals

Petals play tricks with a breeze,
They dance and spin with such ease.
Tickling noses, oh what a jest,
Nature's laughter is surely blessed.

A squirrel hides nuts in a shoe,
As the flowers giggle, 'What to do?'
The bees buzz in a silly race,
Creating chaos in this happy place.

With colors bright, they laugh and tease,
Whispering secrets among the trees.
A playful spirit fills the air,
Where giggles hide everywhere.

The Secret of Shared Chuckles

Under the boughs, whispers are heard,
Soft chuckles hidden, never absurd.
Friends gather round with laughter to share,
Turning each moment into a rare affair.

In shadows, a rabbit slips and trips,
As blossoms cascade from playful lips.
The wind carries jokes, light as a tune,
Laughter rising like a bright balloon.

Tickled by sunshine, the world feels light,
Even the stars wink, sparkling bright.
Secrets exchanged in a joyous spree,
As giggles unite in harmony.

Revelry in the Roots

Down in the soil, the critters convene,
Crafting a party, oh, what a scene!
With wiggly worms doing the twist,
And the mushrooms giggling, none can resist.

A toad hops high, drawing cheers from below,
As ants march in time, putting on a show.
The laughter is thick, a rooty delight,
Celebrating the joy that dances at night.

From twig to trunk, mirth spreads wide,
In this happy haven, no need to hide.
Every creature joins in the fun,
A merry parade under the sun.

Mirthful Moments by Moonlight

Beneath the silver glowing sphere,
Laughter echoes, drawing near.
Shadows play tricks, creating delight,
As giggles twinkle like stars at night.

A raccoon juggles acorns with glee,
While the owls chuckle from the tree.
Silly shadows dance to the tune,
Celebrating mischief, under the moon.

Hearts are light, worries take flight,
In this realm of giggles, all feels right.
Mirthful moments wrapped in a dream,
Where joy and laughter flow like a stream.

Ticklish Shadows

In whispered winds, the shadows dance,
With every laugh, they take a chance.
Tickles float on beams of light,
As giggles echo through the night.

They prance on branches, branches sway,
While cheeky birds chirp jokes at play.
The trees, they chuckle, roots in glee,
As nature joins in their jubilee.

A squirrel slips on a nut so round,
His antics make the laughter sound.
The moon peeks in, a glowing grin,
As happy critters spin and spin.

So if you wander where the fun might flow,
Listen closely to the whispers low.
In giggles and tricks, the world seems swell,
In ticklish shadows, all is well.

Luminous Laughter

Amidst the branches, lights aglow,
Laughter bubbles up, a cheerful show.
A firefly winks, with mischief to spread,
Jokes twirl around, spinning in your head.

The stars above chuckle in their place,
As moonbeams stretch out, a silvery lace.
A playful breeze carries jokes to the trees,
While critters giggle with utmost ease.

Rabbits in bow ties, prancing with flair,
They dart through the grass, without a care.
With every hop, another joke's born,
In this vibrant patch where giggles adorn.

With luminous laughter lighting the night,
The world feels bright, every heart feels light.
Join in the fun, let your smiles flow,
In this joyful realm where excitement will grow.

Sprightly Sylvan Serenade

Beneath the canopy, music swirls,
With frolicking critters and happy whirls.
The trees hum tunes, so sprightly and sweet,
While giggles tumble like leaves at their feet.

A hedgehog strums on a tiny guitar,
As birds croon softly, near and far.
The chipmunks join in, their voices unite,
Creating a melody of sheer delight.

Dancing sunbeams paint shadows anew,
With every twirl, the mirth just grew.
Frogs croak the chorus, so funny and clear,
As nature's orchestra draws everyone near.

In this serenade, let your spirit soar,
Embrace the laughter, who could ask for more?
For in this woodland, joy plays its part,
A sprightly song that stirs your heart.

Gaiety Among the Glades

In sunny meadows, laughter ignites,
Where fables and fun take off in flight.
Daisies prance, their petals so bright,
As every step feels just so right.

Bouncing bunnies, they play hide and seek,
With giggles that make the meek feel unique.
A band of ants march, their antics so grand,
While jokes on the breeze float across the land.

Beneath the laughter, the grass tickles toes,
In this realm of gaiety, all joyfully glows.
The trees wear smiles, with branches so wide,
As critters of all kinds come out for the ride.

So join the frolic, let your heart sway,
In this joyful home, let's all romp and play.
With gaiety blooming in each sunny glade,
Together we'll craft the best escapade.

Breezy Bliss in Bloom

In the field where sunflowers sway,
A butterfly dances in blissful play.
Wiggly worms wiggle and squirm,
Making the flowers laugh and squirm.

A jolly breeze whispers a song,
Tickling the grass, it sings along.
Bees buzzing in comedic delight,
Buzzing here, buzzing there, what a sight!

Silly squirrels in tumble and roll,
Chasing each other, an acorn for a goal.
Each leap and bound, a playful race,
Fleek of fur, a joyful embrace.

Petals flutter and paint the air,
With giggles drifting everywhere.
In this cheerful, colorful space,
Nature's laughter brings a smiling face.

Silly Secrets in Solitude

In the shade where shadows play,
A chatterbox frog croaks all day.
His jokes are silly, a wet surprise,
As dragonflies giggle with sparkling eyes.

A restless rabbit in a jolly hat,
Tells tales to a butterfly, fancy and fat.
He wiggles his nose, what a sight to see,
Sharing secrets with the old, wise trees.

Caterpillars strut in velvet shoes,
Dancing on leaves without a care or blues.
With every dip and a twist of fate,
Nature's joy is never late.

Laughter lingers in the air,
Creating magic everywhere.
A quiet nook where silliness thrives,
In goofy giggles, everyone arrives!

Nature's Comedic Canvas

The clouds wear faces, silly and bright,
Painting smiles across the daylight.
When raindrops fall with a splash and splatter,
They land on flowers, causing chatter.

A painting bird in colors galore,
Sings punchlines from a twiggy shore.
With every note, the trees sway along,
Creating a symphony, joyous and strong.

Bouncing bunnies in bushy attire,
Share laughs that seem to never tire.
Each twitch of an ear, each hop so grand,
Is a tickle that echoes on this land.

Nature's canvas, a sight to behold,
With every story, hilarity unfolds.
In the dance of leaves, the breeze laughs,
In this comedy show, everyone has gaffes!

Laughter Among Blossoms

Beneath the blooms, a parade begins,
With singing insects and playful spins.
The petals giggle, a vibrant crowd,
As daisies wiggle, feeling proud.

A porcupine strums a prickly tune,
While pinecones spin under the moon.
The melodies mix with the rustling trees,
Creating laughter carried by the breeze.

Mirthful moles pop up from underground,
Making faces with leaps all around.
Each dandelion smiles, its fluff in flight,
As jovial memories dance in delight.

Between the blooms, harmony resounds,
Nature's laughter, the truest sounds.
In this joyous, colorful sprawl,
Every sweet moment, the best of all!

Whimsical Whispers

In a land where laughter blooms,
Silly hats and juggling brooms.
Tickling trees with giggle tunes,
Bouncing bubbles like merry loons.

Wandering through the candy aisles,
Finding joy in simple smiles.
Pies that dance and cookies sing,
In this place, the heart takes wing.

Round and round the merry go,
Up and down, oh what a show!
Slippery slides of rainbow cheer,
Every moment's filled with cheer.

Under stars that wink and play,
Where silliness leads the way.
Joyful whispers fill the air,
Fun and laughter everywhere.

Secrets of the Silly Sway

Hidden paths of ticklish grass,
Where even squirrels stop to laugh.
A dancing breeze with playful sway,
Inviting all to join the fray.

Chasing bubbles, bouncing high,
Swirling twirls that make you fly.
Giggles float like happy tunes,
In this land of joyous boons.

Willow trees with funny grins,
Whisper secrets where joy begins.
Stumbling owls and dancing fox,
The clock ticks to a laughter box.

Every shadow hides a jest,
Jolly gnomes that never rest.
Let's lose track of time today,
Where smiles lead us on our way.

Radiance of Reflection

In the mirror of the day,
Laughter bounces, come what may.
Silly hats and crazy shoes,
In this realm, we cannot lose.

Clouds of fluff like cotton candy,
Here, the light is never dandy.
Sunbeams dance on laughter's rays,
Lighting up our funny ways.

Puddles glimmer, watch them shine,
Splashes echo with a line.
Wacky wonders fill the sky,
Where every twist brings a sigh.

Moments freeze in giggling frames,
As we play our silly games.
Reflections burst with laughter's glow,
Where joy is all we need to know.

Revelations in Rapture

In the twilight of delight,
Whispers make the shadows bright.
Laughter's charm, a wondrous call,
Riding high on joy so tall.

Juggling stars and spinning dreams,
Every giggle bursts at seams.
Frolicking on moonlit paths,
Fizzing laughter, happy wraths.

Mystic woods where dreams collide,
Funny wishes, nothing to hide.
Swaying subtly, time stands still,
In this realm, we chase the thrill.

Each moment flows like bubbling streams,
In laughter's arms, we find our dreams.
A carnival of joy unfolds,
Where every heart writes tales of gold.

The Dance of Delight

In a meadow where laughter sings,
Little creatures wear tiny wings.
They twirl and spin in joyous delight,
As the sun dips down, painting the night.

Each leaf is a stage for antics grand,
Frogs in tuxedos take a stand.
Squirrels in hats toss acorns high,
While butterflies giggle as they flutter by.

The daisies sway to the silly tunes,
Tickled by breezes and merry moons.
They wiggle and dance in playful cheer,
Inviting all creatures to gather near.

So come join the fun, don't you delay,
In this whimsical world where spirits play.
With every giggle, the night grows bright,
Join the frolic in pure delight.

Playgrounds of the Wild

In the heart of the woods, where laughter roams,
Squirrels play tag, building tiny homes.
The trees are slides, the ground a mate,
Every step's a skip, can't be late!

Chirping birds start the playful race,
While rabbits hop with a happy face.
The sunbeams bounce like bouncy balls,
As everyone gathers in nature's halls.

Mischievous foxes hide and seek,
With giggles echoing, they're far from meek.
The flowers burst in colors bright,
Painting smiles with pure delight.

In this land where joy abounds,
Every corner holds amusing sounds.
So skip on over, join in the cheer,
Playgrounds of wild are calling, my dear!

Revelry in the Roots

Beneath the mossy, twisted trees,
Lies a party, come join with ease.
With gnomes and pixies, joy's taking flight,
In the depths of roots, the fun ignites.

Bubbling brooks sing cheerful songs,
As critters dance, where everyone belongs.
The air is filled with merry sounds,
As ticklish breezes swirl around.

Jellybeans rain from skies so clear,
Everyone giggles, spreading good cheer.
Each hop and skip is a playful whirl,
In this rooty realm, watch the fun unfurl.

So gather your friends for a wild retreat,
With revelry in roots, the joy is sweet.
A place where laughter never grows old,
A treasure trove more precious than gold.

Laughter's Refuge

In a cozy nook where giggles abound,
A hidden world of joy is found.
With vines that tickle and leaves that play,
Welcome to laughter's bright ballet.

Charming rabbits tell silly tales,
Of moonlit dances and soft, sweet trails.
With every chuckle, they bounce and leap,
In this refuge where fun runs deep.

The sunbeams giggle as they peek through,
Painting the scene in bursts of hue.
As shadows dance with a playful flair,
The essence of joy is everywhere.

So find your spot, let worries flee,
In laughter's refuge, it's wild and free.
With every smile, the world feels right,
Join the festival of pure delight.

Whimsy Under the Boughs

Beneath the trees, where shadows play,
Laughter hides and leaps all day.
Silly squirrels wear tiny hats,
Chasing each other like acrobatic cats.

A frog hops by, with a wiggle and sway,
Knocking on the bark, asking for a stay.
The daisies giggle, the daisies grin,
Cheering on friends in their leafy din.

A rabbit twirls in a dance of cheer,
With floppy ears, it brings good cheer.
While butterflies twist in a shimmering gale,
Their bright colors tell a funny tale.

So come and join, don't be shy,
In the canopy where fancies fly.
With whispers of joy in the warm breeze,
Every twirl and jig will surely please.

Frolics in the Orchard

Upon the grass, where giggles ignite,
Fruit-wielding jesters bring pure delight.
A wobbly scarecrow attempts to dance,
While critters watch, taking a chance.

The apples chatter, their cheeks a-flush,
As bees embrace in a busy hush.
A barrel of monkeys swings from a vine,
Spreading the cheer with laughter divine.

Flip and flop go the wormy crew,
Racing in circles, a joyous queue.
With each tumble and twist, the fun overflows,
As the playful breeze gently blows.

So grab a seat under the branches, dear friend,
Join in the frolic, let your worries suspend.
With fruit so sweet and silly sights,
Laughter reigns in the sunlit flights.

The Dance of Delight

In a glade where the sunshine twirls,
Grinning flowers dance and swirl.
The bumblebees hum a merry tune,
While the sun dips low, a golden moon.

Wiggly worms with a twist can't wait,
To join the jig at the garden gate.
With carrots out for a hop and spin,
The laughter rolls; it's a playful din.

The ducks waddle in their feathery shoes,
Stepping to rhythms, in fanciful hues.
With every leap, giggles explode,
As joy and whimsy share the road.

So let your feet find the goofy beat,
Join the chaos for a dance so sweet.
Beneath the branches where fun ignites,
Life's a celebration under the lights.

Symphony of Smiles

In a patch where joy takes flight,
Juggling jesters dance in the light.
Ripe cherries roll with a happy embrace,
While the sun beams down in a playful race.

A puppy pounces, a giggle erupts,
As wispy clouds like candy, disrupts.
The laughter of children rings out clear,
Creating a symphony we hold dear.

With each silly sound, a chorus grows,
Tickling the air where merriment flows.
The breeze carries jokes between the trees,
Where every chuckle puts hearts at ease.

So let your cares take a soft retreat,
And join the fun with dancing feet.
In this haven where smiles parade,
Every moment is joyfully made.

Mischief Among the Branches

In a land where laughter dances,
The branches sway with playful prances.
Squirrels plot their mighty schemes,
While acorns bounce like rolling dreams.

A jester bird sings silly tunes,
Tickling leaves under bright full moons.
Rabbits hop with glee and cheer,
As giggles echo far and near.

Winking stars join in the fun,
Watching mischief 'til the sun.
Every nook with joy abounds,
In this merry place, laughter resounds.

Bouncing mushrooms laugh and tease,
Dancing lightly with the breeze.
In shadows cast, the mischief hides,
With every step, a giggle glides.

The Sprinting Shadows

Beneath the sun, shadows play,
Dashing swiftly, come what may.
A game of tag, they sprint and glide,
In this silly world, they take pride.

With giggles slipping through the trees,
They scurry fast, like buzzing bees.
Whispers chase them, soft and light,
Each playful jump ignites delight.

The grass shakes with their joyful race,
Laughter echoes, filling the space.
As they weave in and out of sight,
The air is thick with pure delight.

At sunset's call, they gather round,
Sharing tales of the joy they found.
In shadows soft, the fun won't cease,
For they are bound in endless peace.

Harmony of the Happy Ones

In the heart of green, they gather tight,
A band of friends, their spirits light.
With smiles that spread like sunny beams,
They weave together laughter's dreams.

With every step, a bop or sway,
They chase the glooms, they dance and play.
A symphony of giggles forms,
As nature hums and joy transforms.

The flowers join, their colors bright,
In this happy, cheery sight.
With each petal swirling high,
Their joyful chorus fills the sky.

Together they twirl, in harmony,
Creating joy, wild and free.
In the sun's embrace, they celebrate,
For laughter's bond, they cultivate.

Giggling Winds

In the whispering trees, the breezes tease,
Carrying laughter as light as leaves.
They twirl and spin with a chuckle or two,
Bringing joy to the world, fresh as dew.

Caressing the branches, the wind spirals round,
Crafting a melody, a jubilant sound.
A tickle of air, a rustle of cheer,
Unleashing giggles that travel near.

Fluttering softly, the clouds join in,
Little puffs of humor on a whim.
They toss jokes like acorns, wild and bold,
In this world where laughter never grows old.

Through valleys deep and hills so grand,
Giggling wind dashes hand in hand.
In every breath, a smile is spun,
In this joyful air, we are never done.

Giggles in the Greenery

In a patch of bright delight,
The squirrels wear hats so tight.
With acorns slipping, laughter flies,
As turtles dance beneath the skies.

A rabbit hops, all full of cheer,
Wearing glasses, oh so dear!
The flowers giggle, petals twirl,
As breezes tease and softly whirl.

Frogs croak jokes from lily pads,
While busy bees hum silly fads.
Each blade of grass joins in the fun,
Under the warmth of shining sun.

In this land of boundless smiles,
Joy hops along for endless miles.
With every chuckle blending sweet,
The greenery's a joyful treat!

Radiance of Roars

In the jungle, laughter spreads,
As lions sleep upon their beds.
Giraffes make jokes about their height,
While monkeys swing with pure delight.

Tigers giggle when they pounce,
Their whispers cause the trees to bounce.
With every roar, a chuckle bursts,
The sun shines bright, the humor thirsts.

Parrots squawk in silly tones,
Making light of playful groans.
Under orange skies, they play,
Each absurdity on full display.

The creatures dance, a funny crew,
Underneath the laughter's hue.
Nature's jesters, loud and bold,
Their stories of joy in colors told!

The Sunshine Session

Beneath the rays, so warm and bright,
A picnic spreads, a funny sight.
Sandwiches giggle, drinks puff up,
While ants march by to fill their cup.

Kites that flutter laugh with glee,
As children dash and climb a tree.
With every toss, a blooper flies,
The blossoms chuckle, much surprise.

A dog rolls over, shoes in mouth,
While kids declare it's all about!
The laughter echoes, bright and clear,
As sunshine wraps us, drawing near.

Lemonade spills, but hey, that's fun,
Everyone's grinning, all is one.
At this session of sweet delight,
The world is filled with love and light!

Whimsical Wilderness

In a forest where shadows meet,
The critters gather, oh what a treat.
With floppy ears and wiggly tails,
They spin their stories, each one prevails.

Owls hoot wise but laugh at night,
As shadows dance in soft moonlight.
With whispers low, they share their cheer,
Creating mischief, drawing near.

Fireflies flicker, jokes alight,
As crickets chirp, creating sight.
The trees sway back with glee profound,
A whimsical joy in nature found.

Together they form a merry throng,
With laughter echoing, oh so strong.
In wilderness bright, their spirits soar,
Creating moments we all adore!

Tickles Beneath the Sky

In the meadow where shadows play,
A rabbit twirls, just a hop away.
Sneezing daisies, laughter loud,
Chasing clouds in a giggling crowd.

Squirrels wear hats so round and bright,
They dance on branches, what a sight!
Tickling the wind, with whispers sweet,
Every footfall a melody, light on feet.

Frogs in bow ties sing with glee,
Jumping to rhythms from a honeybee.
A party of chuckles beneath the sun,
Where mirth and mischief run and run.

Underneath the sky so clear,
Joyful echoes fill the sphere.
With every tickle and every grin,
Laughter's journey always begins.

Jest in the Jamboree

In the field of balloons and cheer,
A jester winks, his heart sincere.
With pies that fly and pranks that soar,
Each giggle is a welcome roar.

Dancing flowers with faces wide,
Twist and tumble, none can hide.
The sun crashes down in playful beams,
As happiness floats in glorious dreams.

Bouncing bunnies toast with sass,
Frolicking over the lush green grass.
Each wink a spark, each laugh a treasure,
In the jamboree, it's all pure pleasure.

Pranks and games fill every nook,
A joyful tale, come take a look.
Where jesters roam and giggles thrive,
In every heart, the jest is alive.

Mischief at Twilight

As twilight weaves its magic glow,
The fireflies dance, a bold tableau.
A raccoon with spectacles reads a tome,
In the whimsical shadows that feel like home.

Whispers of giggles float on the breeze,
Naughty whispers from mischievous trees.
The moon plays peek-a-boo with stars,
Letting out giggles from afar.

Chasing shadows, they tumble and roll,
Laughter swirling, warming the soul.
With twilight's charm, the fun won't cease,
Mischief abounds, granting us peace.

Under the twilight, secrets unfold,
In every giggle, a story told.
A realm of laughter, wild and bright,
Is waiting for you on this magical night.

Laughter Among Lilies

Among the lilies, where giggles reside,
A frog and a duckling share their pride.
With splashes and jumps, they stir the pool,
Creating ripples that dance, oh so cool.

The sun begins to play peek-a-boo,
As butterflies join for the joyful crew.
Each petal whispers a giggly tale,
In the garden's laughter, we set sail.

Bouncing bees hum a merry tune,
While the daisies sway in the afternoon.
A ticklish breeze sweeps through the leaves,
Bringing joy to all who believe.

In laughter's embrace, the day fades slow,
With each joke shared, the spirits grow.
Where lilies bloom and smiles ignite,
Laughter remains, a pure delight.

Sunlit Silliness

In a meadow bright with cheer,
Bouncing bunnies sing, oh dear!
Squirrels dance with acorn hats,
Tickled pink by playful chats.

Butterflies in wild pursuit,
Chasing shadows, oh what a hoot!
Frogs in mittens leap around,
Laughter echoes, joy unbound.

Sunbeams sprinkle, laughter soars,
While tiny ants march in fours.
Jovial winds hum tunes of glee,
Nature's jesters, wild and free.

In every corner, joy ignites,
Wandering friends in silly sights.
With every giggle, hearts take flight,
In this playful, sunny light.

Nature's Jester's Tale

A fluffy cloud drifts, what a jest,
It tickles trees, nature's best.
Flowers wiggle, waving their stalks,
Even the dirt joins in with talks.

Caterpillars wear their best suits,
While ladybugs dance in their boots.
With each tiny step, a ripple grows,
As laughter blooms wherever it goes.

Rabbits pull pranks, they hop and twirl,
While squirrels snicker, oh what a whirl!
With a snap of a twig, the fun continues,
As rhymes tumble forth like old-time venues.

With giggles riding on the breeze,
Jesters leap with utmost ease.
The grand tale echoes, wild and wide,
Where joy and nature fun collide.

Joy in the Journey

On winding paths where giggles sound,
Each sturdy step brings joy around.
With plants that wear a cheeky grin,
The journey's laughter soon begins.

A bouncing ball of bright delight,
Rolls past creatures dancing light.
With every turn, a funny sight,
As shadows play with pure delight.

Sunshine sprinkles on jolly trees,
Where each branch sways with gentle ease.
In every nook, a chuckle hides,
Where whimsy wanders and joy abides.

On trails of mirth, we glide and sway,
Finding fun in every way.
With steps of laughter, hearts align,
In this journey, joy will shine.

Glee in the Gossamer

In webs of laughter, spiders spin,
Jokes that make the flowers grin.
With glittering dew in morning light,
Each gleeful spark brings sheer delight.

Dancing silks, they sway and laugh,
Inventing games in nature's path.
With radiant glows, the butterflies,
Join in the frolic, oh such surprise!

From crickets' chirps to frogs' bold croaks,
Every sound a silly joke pokes.
In corners where the sunbeams play,
Laughter bubbles, brightening the day.

In layers soft, like clouds above,
Fun emerges, wrapped in love.
Gossamer threads weave blissful cheer,
In nature's laughter, all draw near.

Happy Happenings in Harmony

In a field where laughter plays,
Chasing shadows in sunny rays,
Bouncing bubbles fill the air,
Joyful hearts without a care.

Silly dances all around,
Flipping hats without a sound,
Neighbors join the merry spree,
A giggle fest for you and me.

Tickled toes and silly grins,
Everyone wins, nobody sins,
Twisted jokes on fun's parade,
Memories that will never fade.

With each chime of laughter's ring,
An echo of the joy we bring,
Under skies so bright and blue,
Happy moments shared by few.

The Mirthful Mosaic

Colors flashing, shades of bright,
Every giggle feels so right,
Crafting joy with silly paint,
In this space, none can be faint.

Wobbly winks and cheeky grins,
Building up on joyful wins,
Juggling dreams and playful schemes,
Life is bursting at the seams.

Catch the spark from every smile,
Let's make laughter the best style,
Snap a pic, a quirky pose,
In this world, humor grows.

Every moment, a chance to play,
Creating fun in every way,
From tippy toes to highest rise,
In this art, where humor flies.

Whirlwind of Whimsy

Spinning round in circles wide,
With a wink and giggle, glide,
Swirling hats up in the air,
Endless joy is everywhere.

Ticklish breezes dance along,
As we twist to silly song,
Fools in hats of every kind,
Finding laughter, heart aligned.

Giddy whispers play a tune,
Underneath a laughing moon,
Every twist, a new delight,
In this world of fun, so bright.

When we twirl and jump around,
Happiness in joy is found,
Waves of laughter, soft and free,
Let your spirit feel the glee.

Jesting Amidst the Pines

Beneath a twisted, wooden height,
Whispers twirl in pure delight,
Squirrels chuckle at our games,
Joking softly, calling names.

Pinecones roll in laughter's play,
As we jest the afternoon away,
Echoes bounce from tree to tree,
Nature joins in harmony.

With each giggle, branches sway,
Funny stories, come what may,
Under leaves, we share our thoughts,
Snapping fingers, tying knots.

Forest fun, a joy parade,
With each smile, our worries fade,
In these woods, forever roam,
Finding laughter is our home.

Chasing the Sunbeams

In a meadow bright and free,
Laughter dances with the breeze,
Jumps like frogs, it's plain to see,
Tickling toes beneath the trees.

Silly shadows waltz around,
Whispers of joy take their flight,
Bouncing balls of color found,
Daydreams spark in golden light.

Puppies roll on grassy hills,
Their wagging tails weave tales anew,
Chasing each other for cheap thrills,
As daisies bloom in shades of blue.

In this place where smiles grow wide,
We twirl like dervishes of fate,
Each giggle shared, our hearts collide,
Holding on to joy, we celebrate.

Lighthearted Labyrinths

In a maze of fun and cheer,
Where every turn brings silly sights,
A twisty path, you're bound to veer,
To giggle fits and playful frights.

Witty whispers echo loud,
As we race through leafy lanes,
Beneath the trees, a giddy crowd,
With silly games and silliest gains.

Chasing tails of butterflies,
With sticky fingers, sweet and bright,
Each corner holds a fresh surprise,
Bubbles bursting in delight.

Hold on tight to this escapade,
Step on the path of make-believe,
In this maze of joy, we wade,
In laughter's web, we weave and cleave.

Memories in Motion

Skipping stones on laughter's lake,
Splashing joy with every leap,
In this chase, there's no mistake,
The brightest smiles, we love to keep.

Wondrous tales of days gone by,
Twinkling eyes recall the fun,
Under the vast and playful sky,
With every fable, joy's begun.

Giggles weave a tapestry,
Of childhood dreams and carefree nights,
In a world that feels so free,
Every moment soars to heights.

Dance through time, both slow and fast,
In a whirl of colors bright,
We cherish each spellbound cast,
Finding joy in purest light.

Euphoria Among the Elders

In circles wide, the wise ones laugh,
With stories spun of wacky times,
Their voices blend, a joyful staff,
Creating rhythm with sweet rhymes.

Gentle jokes and hearty glee,
As they share their youthful zest,
All around, we're wild and free,
Echoes of their joy expressed.

Dancing feet on laughter's floor,
With canes that tap a merry beat,
Every wink opens a door,
To memories that are so sweet.

In this whirlwind of delight,
Elders shine, their spirits bold,
Together we laugh into the night,
As life's best tales continue told.

Chortles Among the Trees

Beneath the branches, laughter flows,
Squirrels dance, and the mischief grows.
Flowers chuckle as breezes play,
Whispers of joy fill the sunny day.

A rabbit hops, wearing a grin,
Tickles abound, let the fun begin.
A parrot squawks jokes to a crowd,
Nature's laughter, hearty and loud.

The brook giggles, splashing around,
With every ripple, more joy is found.
Frogs leap in sync to a silly tune,
In this bright realm, all sorrows are strewn.

Leaves are clapping, swaying with glee,
As the sun shines bright, wild and free.
In this sacred place where the light beams,
Laughter reigns supreme, like sweet dreams.

The Enchanted Playground

Swinging high on branches wide,
Giggling children, joy can't hide.
Slides made of bark, oh what a thrill,
A squirrel's acorn knocks, there's laughter still.

See the children, skipping and dance,
Each little tumble a merry chance.
The merry-go-round, a whirling spree,
Round and round, they shout with glee.

Treetop castle, dreams take flight,
Imaginations soar, pure delight.
In the heart of fun, where dreams collide,
Every moment is a treasured ride.

Glorious laughter fills the space,
Nature's playground, a joyful place.
Under the sky, no cloud in view,
Each giggle echoes, bright and true.

Delights in the Woodlands

In the woodlands, a giggle parade,
A rabbit's hop contributes to the charade.
The mushrooms bounce to a rhythmic beat,
Each little creature can't find their seat.

A hedgehog dressed in a jester's hat,
Twirls and spins, oh imagine that!
With each little poke, he brings a cheer,
Such delightful antics, so lacking in fear.

Bubbles float from a brook nearby,
They shimmer and pop, just like the sky.
A playful breeze joins the frolicsome tune,
As sunlight peeks out, laughing at noon.

Mossy chairs provide a perfect view,
Where silliness thrives, for me and for you.
Let's embrace the whimsy, join in the fun,
Under the canopy, laughter's begun.

Chuckles Beneath the Canopy

Under the leaves, a silence breaks,
With each soft rustle, a laughter wakes.
Dancing to tunes the wind has sung,
Joy cascades unhindered, forever young.

A raccoon peeks from a hollowed tree,
With a cheeky grin, oh what a sight to see!
Blossoms twirl, a floral ballet,
In this vibrant scene, surely they sway.

Sticks are guitars, crafted with care,
Animal bands jam without a care.
Caterpillars cheer, showing their move,
In this light-hearted, nature-filled groove.

The branches dance like they're in on the joke,
As shadows mingle, and spirits provoke.
Together we laugh, let the chuckles ring,
A hidden world where joy is the king.

Playtime in the Pines

Among the trees where shadows dance,
Laughter spills in wild romance.
Squirrels chatter, jumping high,
While whispers of joy pass by.

Frisbees fly and giggles soar,
With every step, we crave for more.
The sun peeks in through leafy seams,
As children chase their wildest dreams.

Tickling toes in grassy nooks,
Adventures writ in storybooks.
A picnic spread beneath the shade,
Where silliness can't ever fade.

In nature's playground, moments shine,
With every giggle, our hearts align.
Endless fun beneath the sky,
In the place where joy can't lie.

The Joyful Nook

In a hidden spot 'neath leafy green,
Giggles echo, pure and keen.
Dancing shadows, bright and bold,
Stories of laughter sweetly told.

A rabbit hops with a comic flair,
Chasing dreams through fragrant air.
Bubbles float on gentle breeze,
As friends gather, hearts at ease.

A treasure hunt for fun of yore,
Each silly quest, we can't ignore.
With every step and little feat,
The joy we share feels oh so sweet.

Mirthful moments never cease,
In this nook, our worries release.
Every pang of laughter shared,
A tapestry of joy declared.

Fables of Frolic

Whiskers twitch on a playful friend,
Chasing tales around the bend.
Frogs jump high, with floppy hats,
While laughter bounces, like happy bats.

Tiny feet in a race contain,
Puddles splashing in soft rain.
A merry band of silly glee,
Crafting joy beneath the tree.

Climbing high on branches wide,
With every giggle, fears subside.
Fairy tales in giggly tones,
Wrap our hearts like cozy cones.

In a realm of jest and cheer,
Where joy's refrain sings loud and clear.
Fables born from silly strife,
Make every moment come to life.

Gleeful Glimmers

Glimmers twinkle in the air,
Colors dance without a care.
Chasing fireflies in the night,
Each flicker brings our hearts delight.

A carousel of giggles spins,
With every challenge, joy begins.
We leap and bounce beneath the stars,
Crafting memories that feel like jars.

With whispers of joy and schemes so sweet,
Skating past on dandelion feet.
Each chuckle shared, a spark divine,
In every heartbeat, laughter shines.

So come, let's play 'neath moonlit skies,
In a world where fun never dies.
Together we'll weave the night with glee,
In gleeful moments, wild and free.

www.ingramcontent.com/pod-product-compliance
Lightning Source LLC
Chambersburg PA
CBHW051657160426
43209CB00004B/935